ACTIVATE

Welcome to Activate!

Activate is a 12-week course designed to help you burn with passion for revival. The course will immerse you in kingdom culture and will equip you to live the life of an empowered believer. During this course, you will learn to Prophesy, to minister in Healing, to operate in Words of Knowledge, how to share your Testimonies and how to be a Powerful Witness to others, and much more.

Activate will equip you to impact the world around you through the Presence of God! It is designed to teach you how to LIVE A SUPERNATURAL LIFESTYLE! It is a fast track, condensed study preparing you to activate your spiritual gifts!

Student Participation
It is preferred, and we feel it is most beneficial and impactful, that every student completes the course in 12 straight weeks. However, our busy lives it is possible for a studentto miss a class or two and still complete the course by taking the missed classes the following semester. Students may start at any time and continue attending until they have completed 12 weeks

The Goal of Activate
Our goal is to equip every believer to partner with God in power and authority to change the world. We want to assist you in developing and enhancing every gift you are currently operating in and to discover gifts you may not think you posses. We want Jesus to get His full reward!

The Activate Manual
There are 2 manuals for Activate. A manual is for staff to facilitate the class and one for the student so they may take notes, and keep for future reference and study. The small fee required covers the cost publishing the manuals and administrative fees.

Let's get going and ACTIVATE!
Jim Evans

© 2023 Bethel Austin. All rights reserved

Activate: Igniting Worldwide Revival: Leader Manual

Authored by Jim Evans
Bethel Church Austin

Copyright © 2023 Bethel Austin
All rights reserved.

No part of this manuscript may be used or reproduced in any matter whatsoever without written permission from the publisher and/or author, except in the case of brief quotations embodied in critical articles and reviews.

Printed in USA

Requests for permission to reproduce this work should be sent to:
Bethel Austin
revans@bethelatx.com

Unless otherwise identified, Bible Scriptures Quotations marked NKJV are from the New King James Version® Copyright© 1982 by Thomas Nelson. Used by permission. All rights reserved.

Unless otherwise identified, Bible Scriptures Quotations marked One New Man Bible are from One New Man Bible: Revealing Jewish Roots and Power, Copyright 2011 by True Potential Publishing, Inc. Used by permission. All rights reserved worldwide.

Unless otherwise identified, Bible Scriptures Quotations marked NIV are from Holy Bible, New International Version®, NIV® Copyright ©1973, 1978, 1984, 2011 by Biblica, Inc.® Used by permission. All rights reserved worldwide.

Unless otherwise identified, Bible Scriptures Quotations marked The Passion are from The Passion Translation®. Copyright © 2017 by BroadStreet Publishing® Group, LLC. Used by permission. All rights reserved. thePassionTranslation.com

All emphasis within Scripture quotations is the author's own.

Cover design: Jane Wallace-Bradley
Interior design: Jane Wallace-Bradley

ISBN: 978-1-7345868-0-0

Table of Contents

01	**God is Good!**	page 04
02	**Joy!**	page 10
03	**There is Life in His Presence**	page 15
04	**The Prophetic Gift**	page 20
05	**The Gift of Healing**	page 26
06	**Revival: Part one**	page 31
07	**Revival: Part two**	page 37
08	**The Servant Leader**	page 43
09	**Freedom**	page 48
10	**Pathways to a Supernatural Heaven**	page 54
11	**The Power of Yes!**	page 59
12	**The Value of Honor**	page 64

01
God is Good!

1. One of our most important **CORE** values is that God is **GOOD**!

    - We believe that God is good all the time, **YESTERDAY**, **TODAY**, and **FOREVERMORE!**

    - And we also believe that all that comes from God is good!

    "And God saw everything that He had made and, behold it was very good. And there was evening and there was morning, the sixth day."
    —Genesis 1:31 (One New Man Bible–'*ONMB*')

    TEACHER'S NOTE
    Write on *a white board:* "God + o = Good! Tell of a time in your life when you experienced the goodness of God! When, Where, How, Who!"

    - His **INTENTIONS** are always good!

    "For I know the thoughts that I think toward you, says the Lord, thoughts of peace and not of evil, to give you a future and a hope."
    —Jeremiah 29:11 (NKJV)

    - People often question God's motives.

    - They want to know why He would allow this to happen or that to happen? People want answers when they are going through hard times.

    - God gave humankind the gift of freewill. We have the ability to choose our own destinies. In the garden, Adam and Eve made the first bad choice when they disobeyed God and ate the forbidden fruit. This simple act opened our world to sin, decay, and darkness. It is this darkness that brings heartache, destruction, and grief into our world, not God!

- Like any good Father God allows us to learn from our bad choices. Even the innocent pay for the mismanagement of our free will gift.

TEACHER'S NOTE
God is never cruel! God has no 'bad side.' God is pure love.

"This is my blood. Each of you must drink it in fulfillment of the covenant. For this is the blood that seals the new covenant. It will be poured out for many for the complete forgiveness of sins."
—Matthew 26:28 (The Passion Translation)

- Under the New Covenant and under the blood of Christ all sins past and present are forgiven.

- When the Father sees us, He sees only **HIS SON JESUS!**

- To Him we are **PURE** as snow!

- We are now **ADOPTED** and **GRAFTED** in to the family of God. (Romans 8:16)

- As family members we are loved unconditionally and are heirs with Christ Jesus. (Romans 8:16)

- In other words, God loves us as much as He does His Son, and He wills only the very best for His children.

"If you then, being evil, know how to give good gifts to your children, how much more will your Father who is in heaven give good things to those who ask Him!"—Matthew 7:11 (NKJV)

2. God is **ALWAYS** in a good mood!

    - "He who sits in the heavens shall laugh!"—Psalm 2:4 (NKJV)

    - Jesus was full of **joy!**

    "My purpose for telling you these things is so that the joy that I experience will fill your hearts with overflowing gladness!"
    —John 15:11 (The Passion Translation)

3. God is not only good, but He wants **FELLOWSHIP** with us!

    "And I will walk among you, and will be your God, and ye shall be my people."—Leviticus 26:12 (KJV)

    - God wants fellowship with **YOU MORE** than you want fellowship with Him!

    "And they heard the sound of the Lord God walking in the garden in the cool of the day, and Adam and his wife hid themselves from the presence of the Lord God among the trees of the garden."—Genesis 3:8 (NKJV)

    - Enoch, a **FRIEND** of God, was God's constant companion for 300 years.

    "And Enoch walked with God, and he was not, for God took him."
    —Genesis 5:24 (NKJV)

    "And I heard a loud voice from heaven saying, "Behold, the tabernacle of God is with men, and He will dwell with them, and they shall be His people. God Himself will be with them and be their God."—Revelation 21:3 (NKJV)

4. All that **APPEARS** good is not of God!

    - God gave humankind discernment

    "But solid food belongs to those who are of full age, that is, those who by reason of use have their senses exercised to discern both good and evil."
    —Hebrews 5:14 (NKJV)

- John Bevere in *God Or Good: Why Good Without God Isn't Enough*, wrote: "I saw the words good, pleasant, and desirable and my jaw dropped. Then I heard the Spirit of God say, 'There is a good that is not of Me. It is not submitted to Me.'"

- Many things look good. They may even feel good, but those things, if not of God are short-lived and lead to destruction.

"And when the woman saw that the tree was good for food and that it was pleasant to the eyes, and a tree to be desired to make one wise, she took of the fruit of it and ate, and gave also to her husband with her, and he ate."
—Genesis 3:6

- God's **goodness** is all around us! Develop your ability to taste and see that He is good!

TEACHER'S NOTE
End with a prayer of praise and thanksgiving for the goodness of God!

God is Good

Discussion Topics & Questions

1. How would you explain to someone how you know that God is good?

2. Have the group share their personal testimonies on the goodness of God. What have they personally experienced?

3. Discuss last week's Assignment.

This week's assignment

1. Discuss the topic 'God is Good' with friends, at your Life Group, or with family.

2. What were their objections, questions, general reactions, etc?

02
JOY!

1. Joy is so **IMPORTANT** to God that it is listed second in the **FRUIT OF THE SPIRIT!**

    "But the fruit of the Spirit is love, joy, peace, long-suffering, kindness, goodness, faithfulness, gentleness, self-control."—Galatians 5:22 (NKJV)

    - It is also listed over **250** times in the bible. If it is talked about that many times in scripture, it must be important to God.

    - Jesus said, in John 15:11 that He wants our joy to be **FULL**.

    Why? Because when we are operating from His joy we are better equipped to endure the things of this world. Jesus, before going to the Father, stated, "…and these things I speak in the world, that they may have My joy fulfilled in themselves."—John 17:13 (NKJV)

    - In Hebrews 12:2 we learn that Jesus was able to endure the cross for the joy that was set before Him.

TEACHER'S NOTE
Bill Johnson says that, "Choosing joy is choosing strength!"

"…for the kingdom of God is not eating and drinking, but righteousness and peace and joy in the Holy Spirit."—Romans 14:17 (NKJV)

- We teach and preach a lot about righteousness and peace but not enough about **JOY!**

- "The unwillingness to celebrate before you think you deserve it prevents joy from manifesting in your life. Celebrate because you know who you are through the grace of the Lord."—Bill Johnson

2. As **REVIVALISTS**, joy is our secret weapon.

    - Revivalist don't allow **ATMOSPHERES** to affect us, we affect atmospheres.

TEACHER'S NOTE
We have the ability to change the atmospheres we encounter or to change difficult situations entirely by the Spirit we carry. *Give a personal example of when you exercised your joy and took authority in this area!*

- People have been supernaturally healed through a revivalist's **LAUGHTER!**

- Cindy Jacobs says (on the Sid Roth Show) that the demonic hate laughter. She has experienced the casting out of demons with laughter.

- In one case a man's thumb grew back when Revivalist and Pastor Kevin Dedmon laughed over it, in another a woman's tumors were expelled from her throat when Jim Evans and Eddie Tait did the same!

"He who sits in the heavens shall laugh; The Lord shall hold them in derision."
—Psalm 2:4 (NKJV)

3. Studies have shown that people who are **JOYFUL** experience fewer health problems, have lower heart rates, tolerate pain better, and enjoy overall better mental health!

"My purpose for telling you these things is so that the joy that I experience will fill your hearts with overflowing gladness!"
—John 15:11 (The Passion Translation)

- It is impossible to be depressed when laughing or to remain sad if you laugh for just a few minutes.

- We have a choice. We can **PARTNER** with Jesus and live a joy-filled life or partner with the opposite spirit!

- He left so that our joy might be **FULFILLED!**

- "Do not be grieved, for the joy of the LORD is your strength!"
  —Nehemiah 8:10 (ONMB)

TEACHER'S NOTE

Living in Joy increases your strength. Living in Joy and thanksgiving increases your awareness of God and what He is doing in your life. Worry, stress, and sin clouds and distracts our mind, decreasing our ability to hear God's voice and strains our connection with Him.

---

4. Living in joy is our **INHERITANCE!**

    - Living in joy and love is our **COMMANDMENT.**

    "As the Father loved Me, I also have loved you; abide in My love. If you keep My commandments, you will abide in My love, just as I have kept My Father's commandments and abide in His love. These things I have spoken to you, that My joy may remain in you, and that your joy may be full. This is My commandment, that you love one another as I have loved you."
    —John 15:9-12 (NKJV)

    - What a good God we serve when we are commanded to live in joy and love!

    - Don't marry yourself to fear, anger, and distrust. Marry yourself to love, joy, and peace! We have the ability to choose. Choose wisely!

TEACHER'S NOTE

Have everyone stand. End the lesson by releasing the Spirit of Joy over everyone present!

JOY!

Discussion Topics & Questions

1. Why is Joy so important to God?

2. How have members of the group used Joy as a weapon or instrument to change atmosphere's or situations?

3. Ask why people think the demonic hates Joy?

4. Discuss last week's Assignment.

This week's assignment

1. Look in the mirror every day and laugh for 30 seconds. How does this exercise make you feel directly afterwards and throughout your day?

2. As you go through the week, laugh (even to yourself) whenever you are feeling frustrated, sad, hurt, or angry. Did laughing make you feel better?

03
There is Life in His Presence

1. God created us in His own **IMAGE!**

    "So God created man in His own image; in the image of God He created him; male and female He created them."—Genesis 1:27 (NKJV)

    - Adam and Eve had the privilege of experiencing God's **PRESENCE** in the garden!

    "And they heard the sound of the Lord God walking in the garden in the cool of the day..."—Genesis 3:8 (NKJV)

    - As revivalists, spending time in God's presence is our **SECRET** weapon!

    - His Presence is nourishing to a revivalist, it's like eating a gourmet **DESSERT!**

    - Joaquin Evans likes to say; "We can't say we are about Jesus if we don't seek the presence of the One we are about!"

2. Being with Him is so **EASY!**

    - God wants to be with us **MORE** than we want to be with Him!

    - He is **JEALOUS** for your affection!

    "For I am jealous for you with godly jealousy. For I have betrothed you to one husband, that I may present you as a chaste virgin to Christ."
    —2 Corinthians 11:2 (NKJV)

    - To have a successful marriage one must **CULTIVATE** the relationship.

    - We cultivate a relationship with a friend or spouse by spending time with that person! Likewise, we should be spending as much time with God as possible.

3. How does one spend time with God?

   - **PRAYER!**

TEACHER'S NOTE
Go through and explain each one of these prayers.

- Prayer is a key way to cultivate relationship with God: meditative, soaking, conversational, thanksgiving, etc.

- When we pray it is important that we take the time to **LISTEN!**

- God is always talking! And He will speak to you!

"Then God spoke to Noah and to his sons with him…"—Genesis 9:8 (NKJV)

"Then she called the name of the Lord who spoke to her, 'You-Are-the-God-Who-Sees'; for she said, "Have I also here seen Him who sees me?" —Genesis 16:13 (NKJV)

"And when the blast of the trumpet sounded long and became louder and louder, Moses spoke, and God answered him by voice."—Exodus 19:19 (NKJV)

"God has spoken once, twice I have heard this: That power belongs to God." —Psalm 62:11 (NKJV)

- If you haven't gotten the point by now, **GOD SPEAKS!**

4. **WORSHIP** is another excellent way to connect with the Most High. Corporate worship or individual worship is a valuable and effective way to grow closer.

   - The Father **LOVES** worshippers!

"But the hour is coming, and now is, when the true worshipers will worship the Father in spirit and truth; for the Father is seeking such to worship Him." —John 4:23 (NKJV)

"God is Spirit, and those who worship Him must worship in spirit and truth."
—John 4:24 (NKJV)

- **SINGING** in your own voice or listening to your favorite CD can bring you right into the Presence.

- God doesn't care if you are a great singer or not. Every note you offer up to Him in praise is like sweet incense to Him!

5. One of the best ways to experience God is through His **WORD!**

    - As Eddie Tait, Associate Leader of Bethel Church Austin, likes to say: "Spending time in His word is like spending time with the Author."

    Hebrews 4:12 teaches that, "For the word of God is living and powerful, and sharper than any two-edged sword, piercing even to the division of soul and spirit, and of joints and marrow, and is a discerner of the thoughts and intents of the heart." (NKJV)

    - The Word enhances our ability to discern truth from the lies of the enemy.

    - Every **BELIEVER** should spend time in God's Word **DAILY!**

TEACHER'S NOTE
Share with the class how spending time in the Word has enhanced your life!

- When we, as believers, begin to establish a joyful intimacy with our Creator our ability to hear, sense, and feel His Presence becomes second nature for us. We will begin to experience the awesomeness of His Presence **MINUTE-BY-MINUTE!**

TEACHER'S NOTE
End by urging all to spend time connecting with our Creator in the ways outlined in the lesson. Release an impartation, prayer, declaration, or verbal encouragement, whatever you'd like, to ignite your audience into a supernatural hunger for the limitless benefits of basking in His Presence daily!

There is Life in His Presence

Discussion Topics & Questions

1. How do you enjoy God's Presence?

2. Do you find it a challenge to study the Word daily?

3. What would you say to someone that is challenged in this area?

4. Discuss last week's Assignment.

This week's assignment

1. Practice reading the Word daily, if only a few verses!

2. Record what God says through His Word. What revelation did you experience?

3. Soak in His Presence for 10 minutes each day. What was it like? What did you feel?

04
The Prophetic Gift

1. Prophecy is a **SPIRITUAL GIFT** given to believers by the Holy Spirit. (1 Corinthians 12:10)

   "Now to each one the manifestation of the Spirit is given for the common good...to another **prophecy**, to another distinguishing between spirits, to another speaking in different kinds of tongues, and to still another the interpretation of tongues."—1 Corinthians 12:7-11

   - The **GOALS** of prophecy is always **LOVE**.

   "If I have the gift of prophecy and can fathom all mysteries and all knowledge, and if I have a faith that can move mountains, but do not have love, I am nothing."—1 Corinthians 13:2

   - The purpose of prophecy is to **STRENGTHEN**, **ENCOURAGE,** and **COMFORT** the hearer.

   "But the one who prophesies speaks to people for their strengthening, encouraging and comfort."—1 Corinthians 14:3

   - **DO NOT** prophesy **DATES**, **MATES**, or **BABIES**. Why? Because, if you are mistaken, it can create **UNBELIEF** in the immature believer.

TEACHER'S NOTE
Give an example of when you got a very improbable word for someone that turned out to be accurate.

---

2. The key to moving in the prophetic is **BELIEVING** that you can **HEAR** God's voice.

   "...His sheep follow Him because they know His voice. But they will never follow a stranger; in fact, they will run away from him because they do not recognize a stranger's voice."—John 10:4-5 (NIV)

   "Call to Me and I will answer you and tell you great and unsearchable things you do not know."—Jeremiah 33:3 (NIV)

   - There are several ways to hear God's voice. God can speak to us through **HEARING**, **SEEING**, or **FEELING**.

   - When God highlights someone to you, ask Holy Spirit to give you a word for that person, trust what you hear/sense no matter how crazy it may seem!

   - You will find that it's easier than you think!

3. Everyone **CAN** prophesy!

   - We are all exhorted to love one another by operating in the prophetic.

   "Follow the way of love and eagerly desire gifts of the Spirit, especially prophecy."—1 Corinthians 14:1 (NIV)

   - When you share a **TESTIMONY** about what Jesus has done or is doing in your life or in the life of another you are prophesying.

   "...For the testimony of Jesus is the spirit of prophecy"—Revelation 19:10 (NIV)

TEACHER'S NOTE
Pick a student and release a prophecy over them. Ask for feedback. How did it make them feel?

4. It is important to remain **HUMBLE** and **TEACHABLE** when operating in the prophetic.

   - We don't know it all!

   "For we know in part and we prophesy in part."—1 Corinthians 13:9 (NIV)

   - Therefore, being humble and developing **CHARACTER** is vitally important in stewarding our spiritual gifts well.

   - Ones' character is the base platform **GLORY** rests upon!

   "But the fruit of the Spirit is love, joy, peace, forbearance, kindness, goodness, faithfulness, gentleness and self-control. Against such things there is no law."—Galatians 5:22-23

   - We must carry the character of God's Holy Spirit to remain humble and non self-promoting in all aspects of our ministries, **not** just in the Prophetic!

TEACHER'S NOTE
Explain how the prophetic is like a hammer. It can be used to build up or tear down. Give a personal example of a time when you were encouraged by a prophetic word.

   - Prophetic words given in love have the ability to transform lives and change the world!

5. Prophesy should be **TESTED**!

   "Beloved, do not believe every spirit, but test the spirits, whether they are of God; because many false prophets have gone out into the world."
   —1 John 4:1 (NKJV)

   - When receiving a prophetic word that doesn't feel accurate or is not in-line with the Word of God, it is OK to **FLUSH IT!**

TEACHER'S NOTE
Give the flush sign here.

- God knows everything about us. He formed us in our mother's womb. He knows every bit of us, every hair, every wrinkle, every thought we have ever had and ever will have. If He speaks to someone about us, it is going to be accurate, either today or sometime in the future!

TEACHER'S NOTE
Explain how to discern prophecy properly. Explain why it is acceptable to discard a word.

- Some prophetic words may be somewhat confusing at first. In this case it may be wise to **file it away** and ask Holy Spirit to reveal the truth of the word, if there is any, at a later date.

TEACHER'S NOTE
Give an example from your experience regarding the above.

- When learning to prophesy and while practicing within *Activate class*, it is **OK** to make **MISTAKES!** This class is a Safe Place to practice your gifts!

- God loves it when we take **RISKS** in the service of His children!

- But taking risks requires **FAITH** and **TRUST!**

- By not sharing what God has given you to share, you are sitting on His glory. But by sharing what He has given you to share you are releasing His glory and truth to the world!

TEACHER'S NOTE
Close by having everyone try 'popcorn' prophecy at their tables (after you explain what popcorn prophecy is). The Facilitators will take over from here.

The Prophetic Gift

Discussion Topics & Questions

1. How should the prophetic be used?

2. Why is it important to test a **prophetic word**?

3. Pick a student from your group and give them a prophetic word. Ask how it impacted them.

4. Take two minutes and give a prophetic word to a partner, then switch. Ask for feedback.

5. Discuss last week's Assignment.

This week's assignment

1. Practice Hearing from God

    - Get into a quiet place with a pen and pad
    - Ask God to speak to you
    - Immediately write down the first thing you hear or sense, even if you're not sure.

2. Do the above 2-3 times this week

3. Write down your thoughts and feelings to share with your group

05
The Gift of Healing

1. Jesus healed **EVERYONE** who came to Him

   "But when Jesus knew it, He withdrew from there. And great multitudes followed Him, and He healed them all!"—Matthew 12:15 (NKJV)

   - Jesus healed **ANYTIME** and **ANYWHERE**! He healed from a distance (the Centurion's servant), from the grave (Lazarus), in doors or out!

   - Jesus healed **ALL** who came to Him and He is still healing today! Why wouldn't He? He wants us healed just as much today as He did over 2000 years ago!

   TEACHER'S NOTE
   None of us know how to heal, BUT we have access to the One who does.
   I'm just glad to be the Great Physician's assistant!

   - We must remember this simple rule: God heals and the devil destroys! Our job is to partner with the Holy Spirit and **RELEASE** His love through prayer!

2. We should **EXPECT RESULTS** when we pray for the sick!

   - There is no formula for healing. People have been healed during worship. People have been healed by simply entering into His presence, while praying, or by walking past a room where the saints are pulling down upon the Kingdom!

   - And while there is no set formula for healing, expectation is an important element. You can't expect something to happen if you don't have **FAITH** that it will!

- Healing is a **GIFT** that God has given freely to us for the body of Christ!

In Matthew 10:8 Jesus says, "You must continually heal sicknesses, raise the dead, cleanse lepers, cast out demons: you took freely, you must now give freely." (ONMB)

- This statement is both an authorization and a command. The authorization is implicit and, in this translation, the command is obvious. **It is not a request!**
- Jesus is not asking His followers to heal but He is saying we **"must"** heal!

TEACHER'S NOTE
He would not command us to carry out a commission if we were not authorized to do so!

James 5:15-16 states, "And the prayer of faith will save the sick, and the Lord will raise him up. And if he has committed sins, he will be forgiven. Confess your trespasses to one another, and pray for one another, that you may be healed. The effective, fervent prayer of a righteous man avails much." (NKJV)

- When praying for others with a sincere heart, the prayers we release often rebound to us, making us the recipient of the prayer, as well!
- When **JOB** prayed for others his health improved!
- Every prayer you release goes before the Father

TEACHER'S NOTE
Revelations 8:4 says, "And the smoke of the incense, with prayers of the saints, ascended before God from the angel's hand."

---

3. You are **ANNOINTED** to operate in the spiritual gifts!

   "But you have an anointing from the Holy One..."—1 John 2:20 (NKJV)

   "But the anointing which you have received from Him abides in you..."
   —1 John 2:27, (NKJV)

   - The question is, do we **BELIEVE** it! Do we walk in the belief that as friends of God and as heirs to the Kingdom, that we are anointed to pray for the sick?

   - Many well-meaning Christians pray for others and for themselves but have no expectation that any thing will happen.

   - And when nothing **seems** to happen we find comfort in the misconception that, "I just don't have that strong of an anointing." We think that only the famous ones have that anointing, not me!

   - Bill Johnson, Randy Clark, or Joaquin Evans will admit that they prayed for more people that did not get an immediate healing, by far, than those that did.

   - Breakthrough comes from continuing to have faith and continuously crossing that **CHICKEN LINE**!

   - Just like physical exercise will strengthen our muscles, exercising our spiritual gifts will increase our anointing!

   - Activate your gifts through prayer and taking action. Remember the command from Jesus wasn't a request!

TEACHER'S NOTE

Have the class repeat the words of Christ, "You must continually heal sicknesses, raise the dead, cleanse lepers, cast out demons: you took freely, you must now give freely. (Matthew 10:8). *Demonstrate how to pray for the sick with a partner!*

The Gift of Healing

Discussion Topics & Questions

1. Who is authorized to pray for the sick?

2. If God wants everyone healed, then why do some people not receive healing when we pray for them?

3. Why do you think Jesus felt so strongly about us praying for one another?

4. Discuss last week's Assignment.

This week's assignment

1. Pray for someone you know to be healed! Write down the experience. What happened? How did you feel during and after? How did they feel during and after?

2. Pray for a stranger to be healed! Write down the experience. What happened? How did you feel during and after? How did they feel during and after?

06
What Exactly Is REVIVAL? *Part one*

1. The root word for revival is **REVIVE!**

    - To revive is to return to life, consciousness, vigor, strength, or a **FLOURISHING** condition.

    - "Revival: an **awakening** in a church or community..." —Joaquin Evans.

TEACHER'S NOTE

In other words, revival is when a growing number of people are growing in their knowledge, intimacy, and passion for the presence of Jesus!

"So continuing daily with one accord in the temple, and breaking bread from house to house, they ate their food with gladness and simplicity of heart, 47 praising God and having favor with all the people. And the Lord added to the church daily those who were being saved."—Acts 2:46-47 (NKJV)

2. One element of revival is an **OUTPOURING!**

    - An outpouring of the **SPIRIT OF GOD** on His people!

"And it shall come to pass afterward
That I will pour out My Spirit on all flesh;
Your sons and your daughters shall prophesy,
Your old men shall dream dreams,
Your young men shall see visions.
And also on My menservants and on My maidservants
I will pour out My Spirit in those days."
—Joel 2:28-29 (NKJV)

- An outpouring can be a **SUDDEN OCCURRENCE** in an individual (personal) or a group (communal) (as in a release of glory-gold dust, jewels, indoor rain, etc.) or it can be a gradual awareness of His presence (as in the feeling one gets when listening to a worship song, or after reading a certain bible verse, or when a speaker says something that awakens one's spirit).

TEACHER'S NOTE
If you have any personal experience in this area share it with the class!

3. Revival starts with a deep, unrelenting **hunger** for **MORE** of **GOD**!

    - It can come through the hungry hearts of a **GROUP** or it can come through the **INSATIABLE** heart of an **INDIVIDUAL!**

    - The **FIRST-CENTURY** revival came with the birth of Jesus! Jesus set revival fires wherever He went!

    - The corporate hunger of the apostles brought the gift of the Holy Spirit in Acts 2!

    - "When the Day of Pentecost had fully come, they were all with one accord in one place. And suddenly there came a sound from heaven, as of a rushing mighty wind, and it filled the whole house where they were sitting. Then there appeared to them divided tongues, as of fire, and one sat upon each of them. And they were all filled with the Holy Spirit and began to speak with other tongues, as the Spirit gave them utterance."—Acts 2: 1-4 (NKJV)

TEACHER'S NOTE
Give an example of when you were filled with the Holy Spirit or an example when Holy Spirit fell heavily upon a meeting. What were the conditions? What were people doing (or not doing).

4. Attributes of a **SPIRIT-FILLED** **REVIVALIST**:

    - **SURRENDER**!

        - A genuine, sincere, heart-felt act of surrender is **ESSENTIAL** to host the Holy Spirit!

        - A revivalist must lay down his or her ambitions before the love of Jesus! To be a Christian (a Christ follower), means to follow Christ, not just when it conveniently fits our timetable or when it neatly conforms to what we planned to do anyway.

        - Joaquin Evans likes to say, "We are always looking for something good to do for God and asking God to bless it, when what we should be doing is looking for what God is already blessing and start partnering with Him to do that!"

    - **RELATIONSHIP!**

        - Relationship is important in knowing who we are and Whose we are.

    "And a voice from heaven said, "This is my Son, whom I love; with him I am well pleased."—Matthew 3:17 (NIV)

    - When the Father announced that He loved Jesus, He established a lasting relationship with Him (it was already established, of course. The pronouncement was more for our benefit than His)!

    - How many times are we told in scripture that we are loved and cherished? But the question is, do you **BELIEVE** it?

TEACHER'S NOTE
Give an example of how you maintain your relationship with God.

5. But the most important attribute of all is **LOVE**!

    - God doesn't just love—He is love!

    - When asked what the greatest commandment in the law was, this is what He answered:

    "Jesus said to him, 'You shall love the Lord your God with all your heart, with all your soul, and with all your mind.' This is the first and great commandment. And the second is like it: 'You shall love your neighbor as yourself.' On these two commandments hang all the Law and the Prophets."
    —Matt: 22:37-40 (NKJV)

    - What the Lord was saying to them was that operating in love and from love supersedes everything! He referred to the law and to the prophets because that was all the people of the time had. Though He was slowly changing their paradigm to receive Holy Spirit in the near future, that was their frame of reference at the time. Hallelujah!

    - In 1 Corinthians 13 the Apostle Paul teaches us that love is more Important than any spiritual gift. He teaches that love **NEVER** fails!

    - Love is the universal glue that binds all of creation. If we are truly in Christ, then we must love all of creation and allow His love to flow through us!

TEACHER'S NOTE
End by releasing the love of God over the class and pray for an increase in our capacity to love like He does!
*See more elements of the spirit-filled revivalist in revival II

What exactly is REVIVAL? *Part One*

Discussion Topics & Questions

1. What does revival personally mean to you?

2. Has anyone experienced an **outpouring** of God's Spirit in his or her lives?

3. Has anyone been part of an **outpouring** corporately?

4. Are there any other elements to revival or a Spirit-filled life that perhaps weren't mentioned during the lesson?

This week's assignment

1. Talk to two people you know about revival and what that means to them.

2. Tell someone (other than your spouse or children) this week that you love him or her! How did that make them feel? How did it make you feel?

07
What Exactly Is REVIVAL? *Part two*

1. In our previous look at revival we defined the term as:

   - An outpouring of the Spirit of God on His people!

   - We also examined the root word of revival: To revive is to return to life, consciousness, vigor, strength, or a flourishing condition.

   - Now that we have an understanding of what this phenomena of God is, let's take a look at some of the major revivals in **RECENT** history

2. The **WELSH** revival!

   - In 1904 revival broke out in Wales.

   - In two years roughly 150,000 new converts filled the local churches.

   - 5 years later 82.5% of that number **REMAINED** actively worshipping in their churches!

   - Many of the others moved to greener pastures in the West.

TEACHER'S NOTE
Wales was a difficult place to thrive at the time. Coal-mining was the dominant industry and claimed many lives of the workers either through accidents or disease. The earth was stony and mountainous. Due to extreme hardship many left for Canada, USA, and Australia.

   - Some historians believe that as many as **250,000** people were actually born-again from 1904 to 1905. Not all joined established churches and therefore were not recorded.

- An unknown bible student named Evan Roberts is credited as the **FATHER** of the Welsh Revival.

- He went from a virtually unknown to the most talked about man in Wales in two weeks!

- Why Evan Roberts? Because he was willing to abandon his own **AGENDA** to follow God's.

TEACHER'S NOTE
Roberts was an unknown bible school student who heard the voice of God and followed it. When he left school to preach and release revival in his country, he had only been a student for two months!

- Most taverns went bankrupt.

- Crime was cut in half resulting in many police forces laying off half their officers. Jails **CLOSED**.

- One police department started sending their officers out as singing quartets because they had nothing better to do!

3. The **AZUSA STREET REVIVAL!**

- In 1906, William Seymour and a group of Caucasian and African-American believers began holding meetings in a small house on **BONNIE BRAE** Street in Los Angeles.

TEACHER'S NOTE
Seymour was the son of a slave and had lost an eye to small pox.

- As Seymour taught from the Book of Acts, people began to receive the Holy Spirit!

- Shortly the crowds grew so large that they had to move to a barn on Azusa Street where they witnessed thousands of healings and other miracles including, a **GLORY CLOUD** filling the hall on several occasions and spiritual flames emanating from the building so high that people from miles away saw the flames with their natural eyes called the fire department.

- There were roughly a dozen major Christian denominations birthed out of Azusa Street and approximately **600 MILLION** people can trace the beginnings of their denomination's origins to Azusa Street as the movement spread throughout the world.

4. **FURTHER** attributes of a Spirit-Filled Revivalist:

    - **IDENTITY**!

    When Father stated, "This is My Son…" He established His relationship with Jesus. Have we not been adopted into the family of God? Are we not heirs? Do we not have the right to cry out "Abba, Father?" (Romans 8:14-17, NKJV)

    - Every revivalist must know who they are and Whose they are.

    - As it was in **ANCIENT** Israel, we have the right to conduct business in the **NAME** of the Father as rightful heirs. Are we exercising that right? Jesus died for it!

    - **INTIMACY!**

    - "…whom I love…"is ultimate intimacy. Proclaiming your love for someone connotes a certain level of intimacy. Father God, of course meant 'agape' love for His Son, love that is unconditional. Even if we refer to the love between a man and a woman (the Greek 'eros') or 'philia' (friendship) it still implies some form of intimate relationship.

- The Spirit-filled revivalist should posses or actively pursue all of these elements, Surrender, Relationship with God and with each other, Identity, and Intimacy to be fully equipped to partner with the Holy Spirit to see Jesus get His full reward.

- But the most important attribute is **STILL** love!

TEACHER'S NOTE
Release the knowledge of their true identity over the class. Have them repeat after you, proclaiming who they are in Christ!

What exactly is REVIVAL? *Part two*

Discussion Topics & Questions

1. Why is revival important in God's plan for us?

2. Discuss the importance of surrender in living the Revival Life.

3. Discuss how you'd like to partner with God in bringing revival to your community or nation?

4. Discuss last week's assignment.

This week's assignment

1. Talk with another revivalist. Pick their brain on their experiences. What did you learn?

2. Research revivals of the past and write a short synopsis on one.

08
The Servant-Leader

1. Leadership is an act of service!

   - Leading and serving are **INTERTWINED!** Ineffective leaders will always want to be out in front of the group but leaders that carry the most impact are willing to step back into the shadows when necessary.

   - Jesus came as a man! He was still God, but He came to us in a physical body with all of our physical limitations so that no one could say that He could not understand our pain and challenges in this life.

   "For we do not have a High Priest who cannot sympathize with our weakness, but was in all points tempted as we are, yet without sin"—Hebrews 4:15 (NKJV)

   - Effective leaders often lead from the **REAR.** A good leader realizes that he or she must walk along side their flock encouraging and promoting those that follow them. They also know that it's necessary to come up behind the flock from time to time to pick up those that stumble or are too weak to go it alone.

   - Leaders should have a broad perspective and a willingness to serve, as well as lead.

   - Serving others strictly for their benefit is the highest form of leadership!

2. Spending time serving the **VISION** of others is good leadership training!

   - Want to be a leader? Want people to follow you and your vision? Then learn to follow someone else's.

   - Serving someone else might mean delaying your own **AGENDA** for a time but the reward is worth it!

- It's good training to learn how to make someone else look like a genius!

TEACHER'S NOTE
Give an example of making someone you've served look good! Make it funny if you can.

- Jesus kept the disciples close for 3 ½ years for a reason. After His ascension, they were ready to lead with tremendous platforms.

- The disciple's ministries have had incredible **IMPACT** that has lasted until today!

- Want to be an impactful leader? Follow the example of Jesus Christ

3. Leaders must be willing to **SACRIFICE!**

TEACHER'S NOTE
Quote John 10:11: "I AM the Good Shepherd. The Good Shepherd gives His life for the sheep."

- Likewise, good leaders must be willing to sacrifice much for the good of those that follow them.

"Just as the Son of Man did not come to be served, but to serve, and to give His life as a ransom for many."—Matthew 20:28 (NKJV)

- Our Lord paid a horrendous price for His flock. He willingly endured the cross for the **JOY** set before Him.

- From the beginning, Father God knew that it would take a blood sacrifice to reconcile humankind back to Himself.

- The sacrifice of the perfect, unblemished Lamb was necessary to free us from the bondage of sin.

- Father God is a God of **JUSTICE.** Sin has to be addressed and the redress for our sin was the sacrifice of his son Jesus Christ!

4. Servant-Leaders must be willing to **GO** where God says **GO!**

    - Serving and leading (discipleship) comes with a cost.

    "Now it happened as they journeyed on the road, that someone said to Him, 'Lord, I will follow You wherever You go."—Luke 9:57 (NKJV)

    - Whether you are blessed to follow an impactful leader or privileged to steward God's people, you may be called to go where you never thought you would go!

    - You may be called to minister to inmates in dark and foreboding prisons, to indigenous people deep in the bush country of Africa, to the ultra poor in the slums of the poorest of nations, or to the ultra wealthy in the wealthiest of countries.

    - But if we want to serve or lead with **maximum** impact, we need to be equipped and ready to serve with a servant's heart, lead with the boldness of Christ, and stay poised to go wherever the Lord leads!

TEACHER'S NOTE
Have the class stand and receive a blessing to serve with an unselfish heart and to lead with a heart to serve!

The Servant-Leader

Discussion Topics & Questions

1. Everyone at the table should share their ideas on serving someone's vision.

2. Everyone at the table should share their ideas on leading.

3. Why is it important for leaders to have a vision?

4. Discuss last week's assignment.

This week's assignment

1. Speak with one of your leaders and ask how you can serve them better. How did they react? Did they give you any suggestions?

2. In what capacity do you lead? It can be at church, at work, at home, or socially? Did this lesson help you to see leadership differently? How have you adapted your style (if at all) due to this lesson?

09
Freedom

1. Jesus purchased our **FREEDOM** on the cross.

    "The Spirit of the Lord God is upon Me, because the Lord has anointed Me to preach good tidings to the poor; He has sent Me to heal the brokenhearted, to proclaim liberty to the captives, and the opening of the prison to those who are bound;"—Isaiah 61:1 (NKJV)

    - In sin we were bound because of Adam's act of disobedience in the Garden.

    - Because Father God is a **JUST** God, sin must be addressed. It must be washed away by blood.

    - Under the previous covenant, an annual blood sacrifice was required to cleanse people of their sins. The animal sacrificed had to be pure, without blemish. Unfortunately, this ritual had to be repeated every year to wash the people clean anew.

    - But Jesus changed all that!

    - He became the perfect sacrificial **LAMB** without blemish (sin) to wash us **ALL** clean of sin **FOREVER**!

    - Therefore, we are no longer bound by sin. Jesus' sacrifice brought us into a new relationship with the Father under our New Covenant with Him.

    - Father no longer sees our sin, but sees us only through the blood of Christ! In other words, due to the Messiah's sacrifice, God sees us as pure, without blemish.

    - Covered in sin, with no way out, other than annual sacrifice of animals, we were doomed to pay for our transgressions and be judged to an unpleasant fate.

    - But we have been **FREED** from the wages of sin by our Savior!

2. Real freedom means freedom from fear of the unknown!

    - We no longer must fear **DEATH** or the **GRAVE** because Jesus conquered them both.

    "I am He who lives, and was dead, and behold, I am alive forevermore. Amen. And I have the keys of Hades and of Death."—Revelation 1:18 (NKJV)

TEACHER'S NOTE
Jesus took back our inheritance from the devil at the cross. *(Explain)*

    - Unlike those that fear death and what follows, we are free to live our lives knowing that death is simply a transition into eternal life with our Father!

    "For the law of the Spirit of life in Christ Jesus has made me free from the law of sin and death."— Romans 8:2 (NKJV)

    - We are also free from worrying about the **FUTURE**!

    "Therefore do not worry, saying, 'What shall we eat?' or 'What shall we drink?' or 'What shall we wear?' 'But seek first the kingdom of God and His righteousness, and all these things shall be added to you."
    —Matthew 6:31,33 (NKJV)

    - Here the Lord is teaching us where our focus needs to be.

    - Focusing on the world brings us into agreement with the things of the world **BINDING** us to them.

    - Focusing on the Kingdom brings us into agreement with the goodness and provision of the Kingdom freeing us from earthly concerns.

3. God wants us free to **WORSHIP** Him in spirit and truth.

    "Then you will know the truth, and the truth will set you free."
    —John 8:32 (NJV)

- Scripture teaches us that the devil is a liar and is the father of all lies.

- Scripture also tells us that liars will be cast into the lake of fire to burn for all eternity.

- If lies are of the devil and are evil, then the truth is righteous and emanates from God.

- If the truth sets us free, then lies keep us in bondage. One lie leads to another and to another and to another.

TEACHER'S NOTE

1) Walking in truth takes character. Character is foundational to true authority and true authority in the kingdom of God translates into kingdom power.

2) Bill Johnson has said, "I am appreciative of Christians who have character but I am impressed with Christians who walk in power."

---

4. **In God's kingdom submission and obedience equal freedom!**

    - In Matthew 6 we learn that we are not to worry about earthly things (money, clothes, possessions, etc.). But we are to seek God first, above all things!

    - We are given free will to choose our own paths in life. At every decision point in our lives we can go left or right. We can choose to go God's way or we can choose to go another way.

    - By choosing to partner with God and to follow His perfect will in every thing we do, we open an entire world of unlimited possibilities for ourselves.

    - In other words, we are free to choose our own destinies, but the first few chapters of the Book of Proverbs teaches us that choosing wisely (operating in God's Spirit of Wisdom) brings life, happiness, joy, and prosperity. Choosing otherwise brings about death and destruction.

TEACHER'S NOTE

Proverbs 4:8-9 says about Wisdom: "Exalt her, and she will promote you; She will bring you honor, when you embrace her. She will place on your head an ornament of grace; a crown of glory she will deliver to you." (NKJV)

- Jesus came and died so that we can walk in freedom. Freedom is your birthright and is yours to claim! Choose to walk in wisdom and freedom.

TEACHER'S NOTE

End the class by BLESSING the class with the SPIRIT OF FREEDOM and EXALT them to CHOOSE FREEDOM and WISDOM in ALL they do!

Freedom

Discussion Topics & Questions

1. Why did God give us freewill to choose our own destinies?

2. In what way does having freedom challenge us?

3. How does living in freedom also enhance our lives?

4. Discuss last week's assignment.

This week's assignment

1. Try seeking God first thing every day for seven days in a row. How did it make a difference in your daily life?

2. Discuss freewill with a friend, colleague, or family member. What sort of opinions on the subject did you hear?

10
Pathways To A Supernatural Heaven

1. "You must regularly ask and it will be given to you, you must continually seek and you will find, you must knock habitually and it will be opened to you, for the one who asks **TAKES**, and the one who seeks finds, and it will be opened to the one who knocks."
   —Matthew 7:7-8 (ONMB)

   - Jesus' message here is clear, if you ask your prayers will be answered. However, He says you **MUST** ask!

   - In order to activate this promise, we must ask.

   - Jesus says that not only must we ask, seek, and knock, but we also must regularly, continually, and habitually ask, seek, and knock.

   - Going after heaven is not a one-time thing. Just like the woman with the issue of blood had to fight her way through a huge crowd to grab hold of the tassels on Jesus' garment, breaking many social norms and laws of the day as she made her way through, we must also continuously and habitually, with boldness and audacity, go after the realities of heaven.

   - As children of the Most High God, His promises are our **BIRTHRIGHT**!

   But note what Matthew 7:8 says: "...for everyone who asks takes." This is not stated in a 'passive' form. It is stated affirmatively, "takes."

   - We must be assertive when activating supernatural pathways!

TEACHER'S NOTE

Quote Matthew 28:19: "Go therefore and make disciples of all the nations, baptizing them in the name of the Father and of the Son and of the Holy Spirit." (NKJV) Jesus is commanding us to go! He is not requesting!

2. Jesus was not a **PACIFIST**!

    - Jesus was the definition of love. He was also humble, but humble does not mean passive.

    - Jesus was bold and audacious in action and in thought.

    - Jesus said, "You **must** ask, seek, and knock. He didn't say please or if you'd like to, He said you **must**!

   In Matthew 10:8, He said, "heal the sick!" He didn't say, "Well, if you have the time and feel like it, could you please go out and heal somebody?"

    - **NO!**

   In John 14:6, Yeshua *(Jesus)* said: "**I AM** the Way and the Truth and the Life..." (ONMB)

    - These were bold and assertive statements! Nothing ambiguous about them!

3. Jesus was on a **MISSION**!

    - He was on a mission and nothing was going to deter Him. Unrighteous religious leaders were not going to stop Him! Oppressive norms of the day were not going to deter Him!

    - Females were considered quite inferior to men in those days. But Jesus elevated women at every turn.

    - Christ-followers became well known for rescuing female babies left out to die at birth because it was considered burdensome to have too many females in one family.

    - Jesus regularly incorporated women into His ministry—His Mother, Mary Magdalene, and Mary and Martha (the sisters of Lazareth)—when women were not considered qualified to minister.

TEACHER'S NOTE
Read from Matthew 10:33-35, 33: "But whoever denies Me before men, him I will also deny before My Father who is in heaven. 34 "Do not think that I came to bring peace on earth. I did not come to bring peace on earth, but a sword. 35 For I have come to 'set a man against his father, a daughter against her mother, and a daughter-in-law against her mother-in-law" (NKJV)

- Jesus is the Prince of Peace, but He has demonstrated to us that we must be bold and **COURAGEOUS** and **ACTIVATE** the gifts promised us. We must constantly cross that imaginary 'chicken-line'!

4. First Jesus said:

    "But you must continuously seek first the Kingdom of God and His righteousness, then ALL these things will be provided for you."— Matthew 6:33 (ONMB)

    Then He said:

    "You must continuously heal sicknesses, raise the dead, cleanse lepers, cast out demons: you took freely, you must now give freely."— Matthew 10:8 (ONMB)

    - It is no accident that Jesus taught us to **CONTINUOUSLY** seek first in Matthew 6 before commanding us to go and do the stuff!

    - Radical-seeking leads to radical-finding and once you've found it, the results are **RADICAL-DOING!**

    - In the name of Jesus Christ, let Heaven Come to Earth and let the miracles of God flow, for the Glory of Christ and for the benefit of all humankind!

TEACHER'S NOTE
HALLELUJAH!

Pathways To A Supernatural Heaven

Discussion Topics & Questions

1. Why does the group think that the Lord teaches us to be tenacious in our prayers?

2. Does assertiveness have a place in the Kingdom of God? Discuss Matthew 11:12.

3. Discuss last week's assignment.

This week's assignment

1. Continuously contend for something. Enter into His Presence the first thing every day this week through the Word, worship, prayer, and a conscious desire to be with Him. Then repeatedly ask Him for something, or seek guidance, or deeper revelation and record the Radical Results!?

11
Power of Yes!

1. One key to unlocking God's heart is **OBEDIENCE!**

   "And it shall be that if you earnestly obey My commandments which I command you today, to love the Lord your God and serve Him with all your heart and with all your soul, then I will give you the rain for your land in its season, the early rain and the latter rain, that you may gather in your grain, your new wine, and your oil."—Deuteronomy 11:13-14 (NKJV)

   - It is true that natural rain is essential in sustaining physical life, but it is also true that spiritual rain is essential in sustaining our spiritual lives!

   - The Father's love and blessings brings us life and brings it more abundantly. The passage above promises us that His blessings will flow through our earnest obedience.

   - If we are obedient, then the only answer to the Father's request from an obedient child is "**YES!**"

2. The most **POWERFUL** word in the universe is 'yes'!

   - God is looking for those that will partner with Him on this earth for His will to be done, but the person He chooses must first say yes to His call.

   - Saying 'yes' is like **KINGDOM CURRENCY!**

TEACHER'S NOTE

In a store you must agree to pay (say 'yes' to) the posted price on the object you wish to buy, you pay the price and you get the goods. It works the same in the Kingdom of God. You say 'yes' to His request, perform the act, and His glorious rain falls upon your head.

- Our Father's love is not based upon our actions. He loves us unconditionally no matter what. But miracles abound for the obedient.

- Gideon was scared and full of doubt when the Lord commanded him to go up against the Midianites. But, after finally saying *'yes'*, imagine how his confidence grew as he witnessed the miracles flow.

- Moses, Joshua, and David all grew in strength because they had faith in the Lord. Miraculous victory after miraculous victory followed their obedience!

- The most important event in human history occurred after Jesus Christ said *'yes'* to the Father in the garden of Gethsemane.

"And after going a little farther, He fell face down and prayed, saying, "My Father, if it is possible [that is, consistent with Your will], let this cup pass from Me; yet not as I will, but as You will."—Matthew 26:39 (AMP)

- He allowed Himself to be placed upon the cross as an ultimate *'yes'* to the will of God!

- His *'yes'* was **TRULY** powerful!

3. God will not **FORCE** anyone to work with Him.

    - God wants willing partners. He will keep searching until He finds the person who will gladly say *'yes.'*

    - But saying yes to someone else's wishes requires a certain amount of **TRUST**.

TEACHER'S NOTE
If trust = obedience, then obedience must also lead to trust!

- Which comes first, trust or obedience? They both do. The more we say *'yes'* like Gideon and cross that proverbial 'chicken line', the more we learn to trust the Lord.

- Conversely, the more we trust the Lord's reliability the more willing we are to say *'yes.'*

Jesus says it best in Matthew 7:9-11: "Or what man is there among you who, if his son asks for bread, will give him a stone? Or if he asks for a fish, will he give him a serpent? If you then, being evil, know how to give good gifts to your children, how much more will your Father who is in heaven give good things to those who ask Him!" (NKJV)

- God is the most **RELIABLE** person in the universe. He wants to give you His very best more than you want to receive His best.

- As our understanding of the nature of God grows and we realize how good He is and how reliable He is, our trust grows with time and our 'yes' becomes easier and easier.

TEACHER'S NOTE
Your *'yes'* is like a glorious praise song to the ears of the Lord. It is better to say *'yes'* to the will of the Lord even if it costs more than saying *'yes'* to the things of the world, which surely lead to destruction.

4. **REPEATEDLY** saying *'yes'* to the things of the world make us vulnerable!

"For we do not wrestle against flesh and blood, but against principalities, against powers, against the rulers of the darkness of this age, against spiritual hosts of wickedness in the heavenly places."—Ephesians 6:12 (NKJV)

- Ephesians 6 encourages us to put on the full armor of God daily to combat the evil of this age. Obedience to the will of the Father adds layers to your armor and to your combat readiness!

- Saying *'yes'* to the things of this world is like trading in counterfeit currency.

- Passing counterfeit bills lead to prison not freedom!

- Say *'yes'* to His love, to His will, and to His promises.

- Saying *'yes'* to the Father unlocks immense heavenly resources and freedom for His obedient ones!

- Follow the example of Jesus and all our Kingdom heroes and learn to say *'yes'*.

Power of YES!

Discussion Topics & Questions

1. Do you agree that saying *'yes'* to God is powerful?

2. Can you think of other biblical figures whose *'yes'* changed their lives?

3. How might saying *'yes'* more change your life?

4. Discuss last week's assignment.

This week's assignment

1. Very simply, start saying *'yes'* more to what you hear God saying. What effect is it having on your daily life?

12
The Value of Honor

1. "It is the honor of God to conceal a thing, but the honor of Kings is to search out a matter."—Proverbs 25:2 (ONMB)

   "It is the glory of God to conceal a matter, But the glory of kings is to search out a matter."—Proverbs 25:2 (NKJV)

   - In the passages above The One New Man Bible's translation uses the word honor, but the New King James Version uses glory!

   - Webster states that **HONOR** is synonymous with glory!

   - In other words, when we honor something we give it glory.

   - But just like the word **LOVE** has many meanings in the Greek and can be demonstrated in many ways and on different levels (agape is a pure, unselfish, sacrificial love; phileo is to have affection for someone; eros means erotic love), honor can also be addressed and offered in different ways and on different levels.

   - Learning to honor and teaching our children how to give honor, and to whom, is essential to Kingdom living.

   - God created the family unit as the bedrock of society. Through God-centered family living we experience love, safety and stability. Learning to honor and respect others in God's Kingdom is the glue that binds us together.

TEACHER'S NOTE
Share your experience when HONOR was demonstrated correctly and/or not at all.

   - But **WHO** do we honor, **WHY** do we honor, and **HOW** do we honor?

Now to the King eternal, immortal, invisible, to God who alone is wise, be honor and glory forever and ever. Amen."—1 Timothy 1:17 (NKJV)

- We must start by honoring **GOD THE FATHER!**

- The Father is worthy of our honor and glory and by honoring Him we learn how it's done.

- The Apostle Paul, always the teacher, included this exaltation in his letter to Timothy for a reason. Timothy, a long time disciple of Paul's, already had this knowledge. But it was included so that all who read it knew that the Father was to be honored and glorified.

"Train up a youth in the Way he should go, and when he is old he will not depart from it." *(The capital W is directly from the text)*
—Proverbs 22:6 (ONMB)

- We must teach young and old to honor the Father!

- Our honor is manifest through our obedience to His will, through our praise and worship, and by the giving of the first fruit of our labor.

- We must honor **JESUS!**

"But we see Jesus, who was made a little lower than the angels, for the suffering of death crowned with glory and honor, that He, by the grace of God, might taste death for everyone."—Hebrews 2:9 (NKJV)

- Jesus said that if we've seen Him then we've seen the Father! Therefore, if we honor the Father we must also honor the Son!

- Christ set aside His deity, was born as a mere mortal, and gladly sacrificed Himself to reconcile us to the Father.

- Jesus didn't just talk the talk, He walked the walk! His entire life was a demonstration of grace, honoring the Father, and how to walk in power and authority.

- We honor Christ by having faith in His word, promises, and instruction.

- We honor Him with our worship and praise, in our obedience to His command to love God and one another, but most of all by living in His awesome Presence moment-by-moment.

- We must honor **ONE ANOTHER!**

"So in everything, do to others what you would have them do to you, for this sums up the Law and the Prophets."—Matthew 7:12 (NIV)

- If we would have true honor, we must give true honor; honor to God and honor to each other. Honor given out of fear or obligation is false and will fail in the face of liberty.

"This is My commandment, that you love one another as I have loved you." —John 15:12 (NKJV)

- Our Lord's desire that we love, cherish, and honor each other is clear.

- Just as Jonathan honored David with his life, and Jesus honored us with His, we must honor each other by living our lives in honesty, in covenant, and by sacrificing our desires to assure that our neighbors obtain theirs. In this way, we all flourish.

- We must also honor those **TREASURES** God has given us to steward!

- Hebrews 2:7 says about man: "You have made him a little lower than the angels; You have crowned him with glory and honor, And set him over the works of Your hands." (NKJV)

- God has given us dominion over His creation. He did not give the world to the angels but to humans. We must honor this great gift!

TEACHER'S NOTE
In the above translation the Greek translation states angels, the Hebrew and Latin have God!

- We must treat the things that God has given us with care, as if they were gifts from God Himself because they were.

- Steward **ALL** things well, being mindful to nourish, replenish, and guard against natural enemies. Love them as you love yourself.

- Moses, Joshua, and David all grew in strength because they honored the promises of the Lord.

2. The **NATURE** of honor!

    - Honor is not understood well and is practiced poorly. True honor creates an atmosphere for God's grace to flourish!

    - In writing the Forward to Danny Silk's book, A Culture of Honor, Bill Johnson writes that many leaders tell him that they also have a culture of honor in their organizations but after visiting Bethel, Redding for a week or two they see true honor and realize that they didn't truly understand it nor have they captured it back home.

    - Honor is not reserved for the rich or famous, for the well accomplished or the well spoken. If a culture does not honor the volunteers (no matter what roles they play) as well as they honor the pastor and officers of the church, then that culture does not have true honor and maintaining revival, if it does come, will be difficult if not impossible to do

    - Honor is woven into a revival culture.

    - Honor **MUST** be ever-present!

    - A man should not show honor at work or at church then dishonor his wife and family at home.

    - It is a public matter as well as a private one!

    - God is the author of honor, which is a manifestation of His grace, which in turn is the fruit of His goodness!

- Just like Coltrane's sax or Clapton's guitar are not the originators of their music but instruments they use to release their creative genius, likewise, God has entrusted us to be His instruments to bestow His honor to those He has placed within our sphere of influence.

TEACHER'S NOTE

Like a great musician's instrument, exalt the class to be an instrument through which God's grace and honor can flow!

The Value of Honor

Discussion Topics & Questions

1. Why is honor important to God?

2. Why do you think honor is important in society?

3. Why is honor essential in ushering in and maintaining revival?

4. Discuss last week's assignment.

This week's assignment

1. Take note of the environments you're in where honor is fostered. How is it maintained? Does leadership lead the way?

2. Take note of the environments you're in where honor is not fostered. What differences do you note in the attitudes and efficiency of those involved?

Notes and Testimonies

Made in the USA
Coppell, TX
03 September 2023